Hunger

Johnny Summerfield
Poems

Library of Congress Control Number: 2013922332

ISBN: 9780985770334

Hunger, by Johnny Summerfield

Published by Summerfield Publishing, New Plains Press

PO Box 1946

Auburn, AL 36831-1946

Newplainspress.com

With grateful acknowledgement to the following publishers and editors:

Solomon and George for including "Any Given Saturday" in the
anthology *Chinaberries and Crows*

"Sweeten the Kitty" appeared in *Askew* in a slightly different form

"Photo Finish" appeared in Mylene Dressler 's *American Stories Now*

Table of Contents

Infinite   9

Thrown to the Lions   10

No Compromise   11

Sweeten the Kitty   12

Satiety   13

Mini Stroke   14

The Caducity of Life   16

Shifted   17

Summer Sleep in Sicily   18

Superfragilistic Barbie   19

Southern Nights   20

Slipping Away   21

Satellite   22

Photo Finish   23

Strangely I Metaphorical   24

Nothing   26

After School Extracurricular   27

Bullseye   28

Before Famine   29

Otranto   30

Simple as Pie   31

By the Lonely Lily   32

Starry Evening   33

Candelabra   34

Blurred Mesh   35

Halfway   36

Ethos   37

Fear of the Flying   38

Imago Dei   39

Mile Marker Seven   40

Scattershot   41

One Day, One Hour, One Minute   42

Thoughts Upon Hearing the Desire   43
          of a Young Man to Commit Suicide

Wedding March   44

To the Dogs   45

23 September 2013   46

Interior Alchemy   47

Live (Dead) Oak, Florida   48

Plugged In   49

Judging Kids Wearing Che Guevara Shirts   50

Growing Up   51

Triggering Town   52

Any Given Saturday   53

In a Field Near My Childhood Home   54

Finding It   55

Appetite   56

Hunger   57

On Iniquity, Fate, Blessings, and Poetry   59

Hunger

"Infinite"
{adjective}

There's a finite number of nouns:
Zero, cosmic bodies, God's mind
The created participants:
Mary, Steve, Andrew, Bartholomew, Linda, Jamie, Ozzie, Dontavius
Fishes, fruits, and all the various flavors
Organisms rolling out past the tongue
Sounds called out solely for making noise
Lottery numbers inked in soy on glossy paper
The door knob I scratch my back upon
Naughty bacterium
Utopian zealots unable to grasp their infinitesimal existences
A nurse with a desire to conquer the world -
An even smaller world plagues us, and as
We look into our glass darkly
organisms on specks of ash, stuck to the bottom,
wave multi-colored banners.

Thrown to the Lions

Under August heat
we wandered streets of old Siracusa
for the scent of ancient blood -
we traced the trenches that had run from the small holding cell
where entertainment must have been kept, and
now some of their bones sure up the mitered walls -
Needs no knowing to hear the terrifying cries
the cracking and splintering fingernails gripping, groping,
frantically they must have clawed,
as their tormentors do now, as play toys of the eternally damned
demons who delight in ripping appendages
under high heat
wanting merely a cool drop of water for their forked tongues --
my wife gets upset at slight mention of the trains that went north
from her city of Catania, in the 1940s,
so that some Darwinian scientists could play eugenic
games with real people -
she cries when she hears a sad song,
so talk of torture, pain, and death really shuts her down
to the point of feeling sleepy.
Our earthly forebears proclaim
in so many words, in scripture,
"Do not leave us Father!"
and I'm not any more faithful, but it seems
I am not afraid of your forsaking me, so much as I am
afraid of myself, forsaking You.
So, sear my heart, Lord God of Heaven,
for your heated seal will dissipate my lethargy, and
keep me praying in darkness
in the dark garden nights of my life.

No Compromise

Sin, a songbird weeping,
flesh that peels,
hellish cultures,
cauldrons of misty minds, and
naked feet.

Believe what ought, and
passion find, as sin
makes consequence, and
with the faithful mind, the supposed unknown
the only way
some feel safe.

Sweeten the Kitty

My father-in-law always jokes that cats taste good
with a little oil, salt, and pepper,
a little tasteless joke between the pair of us.
I tell him I like to have the kitty sweetened,
though he never understands this expression
created long before I arrived to this rat's alley
with my American idiom in tow -
He likes to slap the horse meat in the macelleria, and
say how lean and saporito it is,
and he always hands me a boiled slice
that I keep refusing -
Gianni's parents ate steak during the war,
his father a civil servant black shirt,
while my mother-in-law's family,
with no Mussolini card, survived on potatoes
with a hundred eyes -
when proteins become scarce,
again, and they certainly will, I guess I could
whack a cat in the alley,
spice him up with oil, salt, and pepper,
chase him with soured wine,
but until then, I will pray for sustenance
from some less interesting means
and figure a new way
to get Gianni to sweeten the kitty.

Satiety

a fat word not heard much -
Aquinas and Augustine might have defined it as
something hard to grasp, though
always there,
yet, when I ponder my own
existence, inquisitively,
though never unbelievingly,
I hold my hands out and stare
palms open
with wide wonder
impressed by what I see, and
I ask myself and others,
Isn't it amazing ... don't you find it simply amazing
how God has so carefully wrought us?
My friends think I am a raving lunatic, though
I doubt most of them even recall
this singular highlight in my life, so small to them, yet
so fat with memory to me.

Mini-Stroke

(for my Aunt Jackie)

Sandy's just off a feeding tube at the Orlando Medical Center on Sand Lake, and she wants her lollies that the nurses gave her earlier to practice her sucking. Her flap doesn't work, so she sucks for relief and for the taste and to practice opening and closing. Two of her three sisters encourage her as she sits in a chair; she hates the bed because it makes her slide. There are many in the room, some from church, sisters, sister's husbands, and sister's boyfriends, her second husband's son who suffers depression, her nephew who remembers talking about frogs with her as a boy.

Her sister Angel asks Sandy's daughter to go down for a smoke. Smokers are in tune with each other, like the medical professionals that walk the halls. They just sort of look at one another like two lovers at a party full of adults in heat. They've been warned three times this weekend for smoking on campus. Angel never could figure why they call a hospital a campus. "It's not a school. I don't get it. And why can't we smoke in our own damn cars? They told me to put out a cigarette I was smoking in my own car, windows rolled up." Sandy's daughter cackles and then gets close to Angel and places her face next to Angel's, "They said that the vent you use in the car to vent the smoke out, gets into the parking lot where no one's allowed to smoke." All the sister's laugh, but Sandy sucks her hard honey lolly and tries to manipulate the start button on a stuffed frog.

Everyone in the room gets hungry and there's talk of going downtown to a bistro for a nice coffee and cake after a sandwich. That's the way Floridian's eat in summer: pimiento cheese sandwiches, fruit salad, a coffee or iced tea, and light cake. Sandy's brother, Lonnie's late wife, was good at a nice Florida summer spread before she died of cigarettes. She loved her cigarettes as she sat on her raised and covered patio porch. She was a Tennessee girl, sweet and sour, beautiful and mysterious, never too much of a friend to the sisters though. That's why Lonnie is not here to see his sister. He called earlier and talked to Sandy's daughter. Sandy's nephew speaks fondly of Lonnie with Sandy. Lonnie's lake was the backdrop of their special froggie moment so many years ago. Lonnie has one brother, incarcerated, as he has been several times before, and the other two, gone now from drink and other vices. But Jason, Sandy's husband tells everyone that a full cafeteria meal is just $5, including dessert. A young, smart kid from the city delivers, and he ends up with a ten dollar tip from Angel and a few more from some of the others. The room is stacked full of trays and empty plastic hospital cups and holders. Sandy is upset she cannot eat and is exhausted from all of the commotion, so she starts falling asleep and then catches herself over and over, only nobody is noticing. Then her nephew holds her head and quietens the room. He announces, "Aunt Sandy needs peace you guys. She's tired. Can't we all go and leave her here with her husband?"

Outside, Sandy's nephew watches Angel, his mother, and Sandy's daughter smoke in front of the emergency room entrance, not intimidated by the security cameras, and then vigilant security guards come out and ask the women to clear the space. They ask how far and before it's over, they are down the road at a bus stop, a business stop full of people who get up and walk outside the shed to keep from inhaling the smoke. Sandy's nephew, Angel's son, pulls up to the stop and opens his door. "Get in mom, we have seen Aunt Sandy and now we must get home." Angel reluctantly stamps out her cigarette and hugs Sandy's daughter, then Sandy's daughter blows smoke just before she places her head inside the car. "Bye! Thanks for coming to see momma. Maybe I'll get to see your family soon?" Sandy's nephew nods his head and says, "Yes. Yes. That would be nice."

He takes Sand Lake past his turn and spends thirty minutes getting back to I-4. When they get off the turnpike and close to Gainesville, he turns off for gasoline. After he pumps he pulls the car close to the storefront and then steps back out to get a bottle of water. Angel puts up her hand as he starts to close the door. "Son, get me a quart of beer. Your father never lets me have it." He nods his head and closes the door, and then smiles as he sees an old friend from years gone by. She's stamping out a cigarette as she walks.

The Caducity of Life

In memory of Dionisio Damiani who served in the North African Campaign for Italy and then returned to rebuild Ethiopia

"See none" covers his right eye
afraid of light
digging sleep from the corners,
the left hand in place
propping himself up
high in the branches
near the wide open savanna

"Hear none" holds his young, large, dish-shaped ears
and hears nothing from above him, though looks
as if he does -
feet pointing inward, arm held in a bow shape
scratching his leg
he hee hees and shakes his branch
shoveling fleas and lice into his mouth, with elongated digits
and opposable thumb, loose skin and supple knuckles,
pacified by silence

"Speak none" sits on a branch below, and
jumps short leaps up and down
swishing to the swoosh
of the hot African air
his lips sealed

"Hear none" drops from his limb which was too limp
and cracks his monkey head on a protruding rock -
the other two monkeys scurry to the dusty ground
and gather around, staring at their fallen brother,
and scratch their heads, making sure to keep an eye
shut, a mouth closed -

Then they go back to the safety of the heights
facing the open savanna
as the sun drops below the horizon

Shifted

Owls hoot the long shot, and
Worry not that the sun will drop
On a mass of rollers
Behind starry curtains -

The moon bleeds red
like madness bellowing from sandy throats, and
An impulse
Dying, somewhere,
Yet the moon harbors no words

Summer Sleep in Sicily

Window light flickers
like the end of a reel on an old projector in home room.
My hands rest on cold granite, palms up. The Web
caffé too noisy for sleep,
too hot to close the window,
I twist myself and put
both elbows on the cold stone, and
lower my cheek to surface.
Next door, two pair of feet dance
fancy steps, slow fancy steps without music –
I smile and slobber,
my nerves calm enough to sleep
under the mercy of the fan's rotations
in its dark corner
spinning almost silently.

Superfragilistic Barbie
with regards to Denise Duhamel

Barbie digs me.
I saw her check me out.
Can't let my daughter know.
It would be weird.
Barbie broke up with Ken.
We rendezvous after my wife
and children turn in.
I say the white male is castrated,
payback for our fathers' sins,
though my father never knew
his father, met him once,
an old mountain man.

We play poker, Barbie and I.
I let her know it can't be,
though she does have a beautiful body.
Ken would bug out if he heard me.
I owned him when he was a steward.
My brothers thought it was queer.
What boy prefers Ken
to Stretch Armstrong or GI Joe?
Ken has the babes, I said,
and an airline gold credit card with access
to the first class lounge. He's the man.

Ken thinks they'll get back together.
I make a few plugs for him.
She smiles when I say his name.
She always smiles. Even as I stuff her
Back into the shoe box, slide her
Under the couch. She'll be cool
Until we meet again. Tomorrow's forecast
104° by noon, her beautiful face
already threatening to melt away

Southern Nights

Some nights
I feel the air on my skin
as the smoke beside me
refuses to rise,
and the moon's light sits
like a pin hole
exposing my underbelly, my
modicum of space from madness, and
I wonder how the moon
sits so motionless, front
and center, and
not a star in the sky
not an insect to be heard in the winter air, and
not a sneaky cat to be seen,
yet I know
I know
an eyeball glimpses through
the pinhole, like Ezekiel's hole in the wall -
water fills my aveola, and
tears fill my eyeballs
until I get smart and move back inside
where the walls are riddled in small patches of putty.

Slipping Away

She stares beyond the curtains she had to have, and
sees them wandering where they promised
not to tread,
beneath the date tree they lose her, and
get away across the backs
of others' yards -
the guilt, the thought of leaving, tugging at his gimpy
shoulder that sags -
she knows how to move him
standing at the window
waiting

Satellite

night images of earth reveal our smallness
our scattered light dots in a huge black mass -
there's a lot of green on a county road in Mississippi,
but at night there's a lot of black emptiness and insect song,
flood lights of catfish farms and parking lot lights of gambling joints, and
scattered, old pick up trucks

Photo Finish

Stopping by my office at 1:58 in the afternoon, en route to my only summer class, the English Department Secretary pops in and says, "Look at this!" In the photo she is holding out to me is a healthy-looking older man sitting in a chair, the sole of one foot propped up, showing off a white sock with a small hole. I wonder what to say only briefly before she says, "It's my dad."

She smiles. Her hands, though, clench the sides of her navy pants, and then she quickly retrieves the photo. He was from Mobile, he and his wife. The wife an attractive stepmother, behind him to his right, hand on his shoulder, a little stern in the face. The picture was taken a few days before his death.

"He looks great in the photo," I say, and she agrees with a drawled "Yeah," then holds out a second relic, a sealed box. After a moment she seems to think better of this and pulls the box back toward her again, opening it to reveal a Timex Expedition watch with a metal wristband. She tells me her father wore it the day he died, just as I'm reaching out to touch its surface. She puts her hand close to the dial, as if uncertain. I can feel the warmth of her hand and the oils of his body as it slides into my palm. Stuck inside the crevices on the back of the case are tiny grains of sand. It's easy to imagine him working in the yard, "clipping the hedges and mowing the lawn," she says, generally enjoying the life of retirement. She says something about another object in the paper box but my mind is still fixed on the watch, clicking away. Then she nods and lets me know my time for holding the piece has expired. Turning my body I say, "Thank you for sharing these things," and she, teary-eyed, absolutely proud of her prized possessions, smiles and departs my office as fast as she had come in. The clock reads 2:01.

Strangely I Metaphorical

Words, stacked cars in a junk yard,
right flat in the middle of a cotton field, and
people rolling past from Moultrie to Albany
gaze at the crinkled K,
and the P in a hazy retro pink that's faded from stare -
Then there are ones in lined parking spaces
in neighborhoods dwelt in by the famous
packed, marked, chock full
with regrets
oppression
experience borrowed or molested,
lifestyles in some fancy borough
where cheese costs as much as a six pack of imported beer,
or bounding rooftops in some swanky Parisian neighborhood
or in various hotel lobbies around the globe,
words reading books on self-fulfillment, and
the twelve steps to get back to the bare basics of the alphabet,
visions of double spaced letters hanging above blackboards
as little children file in with their mommy-packed lunches
red cheeks from weather and embarrassment -
Or words lying around on dinner tables,
oily from being touched so much, and
not a fancy, posh poet-like word to be found, only
HUD house and mud hut, and
their one night weekly trains rail by
opened wooden windows with steel mesh screens
no A/C, but a garden
like Amazonian rain forest
water feature included, and the school bus driver
who wears a fedora and leaves them just to hear all the other
lower case letters and words laugh, and
there are no cell phones with strange new words,
no games on the screens that have etched the words he feels
as he walks to school alone, and no imagination
about the world of words,

only a pyroclastic mind, a yo-yo up and down
a clown: face on,
face off,
face on,
face off,
hornet stings and bullet wings
stab wounds
seven bullies
alcohol on a breath too familiar,
but the good and the bad and the unique and the sad
words, and all the new words
all gather from all over, and
regardless of the horrible gossip
they keep their strength
their posits and nuances, and
their freedom to be writ by whatever hand may try them, and
they feel the grace of God's strong hand once again
who gave them their right to exist
right outta nothing.

Nothing

He weighed nothing, then
decided to switch to business math -
brain cells dead from constant, tiny
glue tubes of irony, and
the idiot followed,
zombified in his corner -
things would not turn out well
before the Chevy -
eating the leftovers
sitting there
begging for rolls,
his belly churned -
Anything.
There's a poem
though no one tries to figure out what it is, and
perhaps it was human a while
a wise guy maybe
guts hanging out
wanting a slow death under the house
not wanting to face the shame -
They went in and pulled him out, and as he cried
like he'd been spanked by the buckle,
he sat quietly in the well-manicured grass
gripping the turf with white knuckles.

After School Extracurricular

Small martial artists swarm around their too proud parents, waiting,
as their smaller peers are tested
beyond the counter top that separates each class -
micro-ninja black-belted five year olds
too small to pee on their own, and I'm jealous for a moment,
maybe because I dropped Scouts, and the Air Force, and the career
I really wanted, but couldn't quite achieve -
a retreat to the car,
I suck cheddar cheese straws and sip cherry-flavored soda, as
a little wannabe ninja girl with a green belt looks in at me
through the driver's side window.

Bullseye

Her true allegiance was to Howard, a man she married young and sexed even younger. She controlled him early on, possessing him. He rarely met friends after work – all he could ponder was her scent, her bosom. That was until he found Carolyn, a forty-something up the street. Of course, he was forty by the time he had met her, he watched her as she shot arrows at a target stuffed with coarse bedding hay, she never once missed her mark. Until her George caught her and Howard boinking in the sitting room – what angered him most was the caramel they got on his lamb wool shag he'd bought in England years ago. "It's ruined," he said, as he loaded the lamb skin into his Miata and rushed over to the 30 minute dry cleaners, sending off a, "Better be gone when I get back, Carolyn," which set her to crying, and Howard, unable to comfort her in her loss of George, shot several arrows high into the sky in her back yard and tried over and over to place himself under each. Carolyn came out, drew her recurve bow forcefully back like a Trojan archer and shot an arrow through Howard's neck. He placed his hand over the hole to stop the light shining through, and then slumped to his knees. Howard's wife drove by as Carolyn drug him toward the garage, and she rolled down her window. "Is that man, okay?"

Carolyn swallowed hard and said, "It seems he has lost his way, and then he collapsed from heat stroke, but his pulse is fine." Howard's wife sat silent a second or two - "So you're a nurse then?"

"No," she said, "I just know how to check for vital signs." "I see," she said, as she rolled her window up and drove on down the road toward home.

Before Famine

(A poem in support of farming with no thought given to Wendell Berry)

Yeomen cut below this crust,
   with a dozen children in rows a must -
Honor by hard work, the credo read,
   and work it was and then the bread.
Not all were Munsters, Corks, or Kerrys
   who sought their fat with every ferry.
Most were Manleys, Killeens, and Garretts
   that could not hide when chased by ferrets.
Sun up, sun down, they dragged the earth,
   sent word home when wives gave birth.
They tilled the ground when tempted to sway
   and thanked the Lord for each long day.
After, made merry, in beards of suds, and
   celebrated hearty in filthy duds.
No hose to wash their mud-caked boots,
   their little Johnnys played no flutes.
They fell down fast, and found their place,
   then woke once more to catch the pace.
A world by farming, lost in time -
   may one day be, as before, sublime.

Otranto

I never did dive off the cliff feet first
as I struggled to balance my body, as
the young Italian boys sliced the water head first,
screaming as their heads popped back.
Their uncle, a retired medical doctor,
an eccentric fellow, their purse,
laughed often, and gave instruction, yet never dove himself, and
when the swimming ended
his youngest nephew, a handsome, though drawn up fellow,
played classical piano on the baby grand -
his playing heard from the cellar
as the doctor looked over case upon case of dusty wine, none too new,
turning bottles in racks and wiping off
dust and calling out years,
though I knew nothing of wine, yet I found
it all so interesting
what one year meant versus another -
he ended up choosing an unlabeled green bottle of a deep red, and
after the playing ended with something very technical and classical,
we ate pasta and fruit in the garden and talked for hours,
and the next day, it happened again,
before we headed home,
but I never did dive head first.

Simple As Pie
(I am no theologian or apologist)

God never proclaims victory
since it's no contest,
no good versus evil as is always proclaimed -
if evil had a claim in the stake of things
where would God's sovereignty lie,
in the depths of the ocean of protoplasmic aura
surrounding atoms in outer space?
No, there is no competition going on
around here, except in the souls of the believers,
where we wrestle not against flesh and blood
but are more than conquerers
by His Holy name,
but His name must be proclaimed,
our hearts affixed on the ever steady mark
rather than on some shifting and movable target
with hollow innards.

By the Lonely Lily

There are no words on the tree I have etched
yearly,   I would say,
the wr   ong tree perhaps,
But   the same callow lilies grow
six   feet to its left
the hol   low log three feet to its right,
the bik   e with banana seat chained with a rusty
1/2 cir   cle lock with a yellow rubber grip -
A de-barked tree
bald but free, so
I rub on its trunk
to feel the small indentation,
the hollowed out symbol

Starry Evening

The children sit with us on the deck
Counting stars as the ancient mariners did.
Orange coals pop open steamy oysters
Spread out on a tin sheet –
I remember collecting oysters, walking the beds at low tide
In cowboy boots
Alongside a johnny boat, and
Camping, with fires ablaze, lighting the white caps
Along the gray sand beach –
In my mind, then, the lights atop the Crystal River power plant
Appeared as buoys afloat in the North Sea
Barely illuminating German subs. But since,
I've walked until the edge of loneliness sometimes
And I have looked as far as the eye can
See, along the gorgeous shorelines of Sicily,
From where I could see Tunisia and perhaps Tripoli, and
From where I have listened intently for that quiet voice of God inside of me,
The way the counting of these God-placed stars on this deck will
Remind the children one day
As will the smell of green oyster shells as they fizz over coal fire.

Candelabra

Medieval candelabra cast wiry shadows
some miserly, some distorted, some superior, and
each a study of light
in this gargantuan monastery once well-ordered and clean -
its failures indicated
by the huge, cracked walls

due euro per macchiato
direttore, dottore

late this afternoon
a shooter
will shoot the wrong person,
the wrong person will suffer, on Via Dante,
just outside, and still
tonight, many men will love their wives in distrust,
after coming home with discharge upon their clothing, and
their teen daughters will be warming
their arms with heroine on cold park benches, and

lonely, hungry boys will sit staring from far walls,
- though not in this monastery which will be locked -
and think of prayers and shouts silenced now for many years, and
with the smell of sea water, and
the itch that will not be scratched, by the drunken homeless man,
or the silence
got at, or the winds, and

the winds will not sweep these grand halls
rocking these candelabra,
and in this place, the place the murderer walked this morning, and
where the winds won't extinguish the pain or clean the stain,
there's fierce stillness

Blurred Mesh

In Winter, wooden windows lift easier than in Summer.
Perhaps the heat expands the cheap pine window frames, and
some spots get pulpy swells
where paint peels get stopped up -
after a while the paint becomes thinned, and
a peel cannot be got, and then
the window loses our interest
to the small holes in the metal mesh screen -
not the manufactured holes
but those brought about by bad children poking at things,
widening circumferences by full measure
jabbing sticks and fingers, and
then the mosquitoes come

Halfway

I would tell my writing students,
learning is proactive, and that they
should meet me halfway in the process -
I feel a right relationship with God works
that way also, except
the journey to meet him halfway
becomes impossible for us, and so
He must sweep us up and comfort
us, or our fears would overtake us
at such great heights
His presence to us would
become overwhelming.

Ethos

The gentle summer breeze carries
dandelions, though
the wild wicked wind carries hay barns and the terebinth
on a jaunt, piece by piece,
their sticks pile high beneath broken bridges
downstream -

imagine,
light of the autumn moon illuminating cavernous
bottoms, sated,
in reflections off tight skin,
a deeper and lustier
wiser and weightier deluge -

study the separate parts, and
the earth, parched

Fear of the Flying

Saharan wind shuffles into Taormina,
scalding the tonsils
drawing all creatures to the fountainhead -
I lift my daughter to get a drink, and
beg her to hurry
with a full line of people behind.
As I drink, after her, my head tilts to the right, and
I open my eyes to a hornet with a four inch thorax
hovering like a helicopter -
this anomaly seems like something out of science
fiction, and
no one bothers catching me as I fall back -
as I wake, my daughter is feeding pigeons with her snack
near the old church door, and
the hornet hovers
as person after person drinks -
this monstrosity in flight to their immediate right
watching their slurps
studying their moves, and yet I,
only I, have a problem with this

Imago Dei

Mago! My wife would cheerfully
recite, as she held our son
by his tiny arm pits, as
he sat in the small, foldable
baby bath
smiling and cooing, kicking
up water
then yelling a long stream of words
undecipherable -
My wife always put the bath away
first, as he lay talking, staring at the ceiling
wrapped like a burrito in his tight towel,
then she powdered him up
like a sugared donut, and
then she stood and stared a while
at St. Michael and All Saints Church
towering over the short, dry stacked stone wall
that separated us

Mile Marker Seven

Hemorrhaging country crickets,
cohort fiddlers in meadows of spring, fill the
green scene,
for mile after mile of forgettable space
much more than a trace
so usual
and
for granted
natural stuff, as unwanted as pastoral
verse -
the car's constant ebbing allows a glimpse,
a frame ahead and a frame
behind
but to the side – in real time

it's all a blur

Scattershot

The brain is less than an inch from the outside world,
protected by a thin layer of bone.

The heart is more important than the brain, as it's
protected by so much bone and cartilage.

If the brain were more important, I'd have no hope.
I hear my heart thump as I lie on my belly.

I can't sleep nights.
My teacher never should have taught us to churn butter.

I never took the lunch money.
I never had any problems. That was my problem.

James B. once gave me a Heimlich as I choked on stew beef in the lunch
line. I never thanked him properly.

I never liked running. My legs chafe.
Though I was good at kick ball. All my power was in my legs. "Go Johnny Go!"

My Uncle Rocky had strong legs and a strong heart.
He walked all over Florida at least twice a year.

When his brain died, his heart kept going.
It wouldn't even stop for the morgue.

He saw lots in his days, in Vietnam, and on routes 100 and 441,
filling in the yanks on local lore and wildlife.

And apparently, as he put it before his death, Memphis thrives
                                        on a river, and its city lights
shine on farmers' fields in Arkansas.

One Day, One Hour, One Minute

It was on the news
about a young girl, missing.

My cousins knew her from school.
Her daddy worked with mine.

She just started being a woman
when she met the terrible man

twisted by a bad childhood
wandering the earth

like Fyodor's demons
trying to please his sick mind.

Voltaire apparently says everybody
rational needs pleasure.

That's because unfortunately a wicked priest wiped away his reason
to believe.

Mom let us out less often
afraid he'd be back around

afraid he'd stalk us on the road she couldn't see
or in the woods outside our neighborhood.

They found her in such a way
I blocked it out for years

from my fragile mind
angry with death

angry with adults
sad to be the one still alive.

Thoughts Upon Hearing the Desire
of a Young Man to Commit Suicide

Discharged, he starts,
what does life have to offer, he continues, and
nothing at all offered his three acquaintances -
I guess you're right, they end -

Life without love approximated upon him like sunshine
makes his happiest days ever had, seem sad
indeed, and sooner or later,
downright depressing.

I'd tell him, if I could, to offer up a daily prayer, and to use a diligent
daily reading of the Word, as this
can reclaim a shipwrecked life, and
ward off the pirates of the mind
that might try to steal his gold.

Wedding March

Knees buckle from weight, as sweat beads gingerly caress
his huge forehead -
he starts across the white trail of cloth
sat upon a concrete slab
beneath the park pavilion, rented
for the occasion -

his wife's head, cherry red from strain and anticipation
of the day, of not knowing the way
things would end, finally, she
sits down before he does, and as he sits
like he hasn't sat before
he sighs relief from the gurgling pain -

at a stand, she starts her wailing, her suffering cry
for her boy that has passed beyond
the part of living that allows her to care, anymore,
in a real way, anyway, according to her,
as she feels a new woman will be there, and so
he moves his heavy arm to rest behind her head
on her neck,
so as to keep her hair all together
the way she had it done up -

he never usually cries except while watching movies,
but as the bride marches in in her fatally white adornments,
the brightness of it sends him reeling,
his fat head bobbles,
his hot tears invade his red cheeks,
no silk handkerchief like a real man,
no tux, no real socks,
he finally contains his emotion and looks to her,
her mascara smooshed about by tears -
he starts to tell her, then silence.

44

To The Dogs

Ottoman Turks bred dogs on the blood of children
the savage brutes
tore limb for limb
in unison, their rips, and they never
listened to the cries, only
the ambiguous noises of nightfall coming -
trail to tears,
the tears to the small boxes of meat, and
the drifting downpour.

12 past the hour
her eyes sank a slipping weight down,
with no lifting of the lids, her body
in darkness,
the shredded camisole and bloomers
and ripped legs in black, brown, and nude, lay bare
as she counted ways to silence.

23 September 2013

I saw this morning how in Nairobi, in a mall,
the extremists are getting more discriminating, as they ask victims,
Muslim or not!? -
in a hot seat, asked to quote a prayer for positive ID,
to declare to be Muslim in the way of the gun toters, or take a bullet, and
maybe the world can see now how tough
it may have been to be German in the early 20th century -
violence and hate have a way of sorting out sides,
quickly and jaggedly.

My wife's grandfather decided he would never receive Mussolini's card, and
so her family ate potatoes thrown beside the roadside
rather than buying meat, wine, and fine pastas, as his
decisions defined who he was, to his family and to the world,
though, maybe he never had a gun shoved into the base of his skull, though I don't
believe he would have caved, but who knows?

Death, not the final destination point for the believer, and
most of us share this desire for eternal life, yet
holding on to the here and now as long as possible
seems to be the choice most choose, the world over, and so,
at least this time,
these Muslims were allowed to declare their faith before the face of death,
without any fear of losing their lives.

Funding

Faith

s

t

u

F

O

f

p

E   +   p

r

L

s

e

s

Yet We *Find* rEaSon - < to go on>

Live (Dead) Oak, Florida

Residence helped a little,
though the main train always poured into town, and
back into the past,
with the wonderful hot grill, and
dynamic brakes
squeaking journal boxes
safety rails on and off the track
blocking access back, and
not that it matters, as
my rewind button sticks, and there's
no more locked groove for my dead pan hands, and
my arms elevate to heaven, for this
place matters little, after all

Plugged In

There's no director's chair in this life,
no love seat in pink,
no cabriolet with prime cane,
no silky chesterfield,
no chaise, or recamier, with
the sofa, jealous and embarrassed
by her length and sprawl, and
no wassily or club,
only this rickety rocking chair
with loose rocker timbers
on an uneven porch

Judging Kids Wearing Che Guevara Shirts

Many new voters don't dream of pleasure gardens, or
ample off-road parking,
sheds with foundations and clap board siding,
property lines
limited access drives,
skylights to the master,
fancy balustrades -
they want umbrellas
over a parapet, fully wired for Internet, and
earth bound gutters clear to the coast
so that every little plant in the forest
can get drunk on their water, and leftover coffee, and
watered-down boos -
they might even decorate the street lamp posts in laurel
place mistletoe on their brows, and
enjoy an increase in knowledge; however,
the teeth of their forage harvester
seems to pack their cerebrums so tight
their corpus callosi may collapse by weight, and
they, feeling so fulfilled
with their freedom from religion,
will be allowed more time on their game machines,
their ghost machines,
dilating papilla, 10 cm or more,
frying their lenses

Growing Up

My walking legs have become prolegs,
all stuck to the surface
like a meth head in a Lazy Boy.

Triggering Town
after Richard Hugo

Things need poems,
even the subjects impossible to pen,
so arrested and
slam-dunked, and
the way "therapy" describes process,
a few more times for the coffer
just to make sure it's out,
so it won't rear its ugly face
again, to the light,
to the mind -

Any Given Saturday

Everything seems to be a football game or
tailgating and drinking -
        an old infirm man in the laundry mat quotes
statistics for all of the SEC's running backs
yet has never read a single poem, or so he says -
my only pair of jeans, my favorite pillow, and three
shirts with grease stains
go round and round like a kung-fu fighter
on a television screen, or an orange
peel knifed off at the pulp
like Gio's granddad did with his fingers -
mirage
a rhyme for orange
orange mirage, my peach-colored shirt,
soaked and sudsy, the smoothed combed Egyptian cotton reminds me of Charlie
Pell and Ode to the Gators, and
I wonder why I know this, and
then I wonder who's winning the game that the old man
listens to on his transistor, and
as the machine puts me into a trance
rain rolls down the road inside tiny aqueducts of concrete
like the big ones that drape landscape in Sicily
and feed farmland as it did during the Roman Empire,
and then I can hear screams
from the large concrete stadium on Donahue
completely in step with the old man's jumps -
between the machines, he dances.

In A Field Near My Childhood Home

Dead sky patchy ground
\
distant daubers fashion earth
 \
hold mud tiny legs
  \
no thoughts free from duty
   \
orange set puddle peddled
   \
luxury emboldened
    \
never bought
     \
never given gift
      \
promises no
       \
lies

Finding It

Ground tunnels, covered in branches -
that's where he sees his first nude
on a page of Hustler -
her fair white legs, long red socks,
ankles close
knees spread wide by one hand
the other closer -
leaves dance to their shadows on the ground
like trapped sparrows -
all eyes across his right shoulder,
the tunnel cool, the ground cold,
warmth runs the full length of his body -
then he rolls her up and lets her smoke, and as ashes form,
his body and the ground grow much colder.

Appetite

Not abstaining from the appearances of evil
remains the main reason people fall, and
these people include CEOs, pastors, evangelists, Presidents,
you name it and that kind of person has fallen, and
it can be fun, this sin, involving one's body,
or others', even the thought of it can put goosebumps up a leg, but
the damage sometimes done,
regardless of how lonely or willing the participants,
can be devastating, and
after all, all Christ wants for us is happiness, so
I guess happiness and pleasure can sometimes be divorced, or
separated, and joy that comes from the Lord
brings about full understanding of these things, and
the freedom that can be got will free one up,
all the way back to that first act, perhaps prompted by a magazine
somewhere alone in the woods -
Only, no one is ever alone, anywhere, for
the Bible tells us so,
plus it gets old, feeling like a prisoner in one's own body,
feeling dirty on the inside, and the out.

Hunger

Nervous energy surrounds my native
interstitial
knee knocking knee
private locution
public solution
between God and myself,
no more faith upon a shelf -

He fills me to overflowing
the way no philly can
yet I love that woman who holds
my tired hand,
but only God
fills my God-shaped hole -

On Iniquity, Fate, Blessings, and Poetry

Though my iniquities are many, I am blessed.

I wasn't a Micah or a Gideon, stupid enough to erect idols in silver or gold. I just showed up to church, mostly for the girls, and especially for the cookies. I joined the United States Air Force to escape my hometown. I got lucky. I was blessed. I got orders to Europe right after my 18 weeks of training. Sicily.

Something incredible happened in Sicily. I found art. It was in the square, in the hills, along the roadside, in the field with the shepherd and his sheep and sheep dog, on the balcony of the hotel where I stayed (some 1500 feet above a precipice just outside a small village).

It was in the sea and its environs, in the antiquities of the ancient ruins, and it was in the people. I understood then why it might be tempting to erect an idol—to place something before God as truly important in one's life. And I did that without meaning to for several years.

I met a beautiful woman on the military base where I was stationed, and I found my desire to exist on this earth, outside of the already existing knowledge I had of God. She was my Aphrodite, my Josephine. She still means the world to me. I had to learn to put her after God. She taught me poetry, language, art, and how to live. I had never seen anything like her. It was easy to misalign her in the order God intended.

I knew though that she was my flesh. And she became one flesh with me on 31 March 1987, in Altus, Oklahoma, the location of my only stateside assignment. We were there only a short while before we went to England for four years and then back to Italy.

She never told me to start writing poetry. It just sort of started. I did write here and there as a kid. Most people told me I was good at it. I won a poetry contest at church one time during a Valentine's Day event, and I was the only dude without a girl. Maybe they felt sorry for me? Who knows. I think my mom still has that poem. I will not share that thing in a book. Anyway, I was curious and so I read my wife's poetry. It was delightful. I then started reading poetry all the time.

Though I had planned to pursue a career in Occupational Therapy, circumstances conspired to direct me toward a life of letters. Nonetheless, the blessings of my earlier intention continue to inform my life and my understanding of the world. Though I'd never wish to repeat the experience, I was blessed to spend four hours with an elderly woman whose tears did not cease. During the sleepless night that followed, I came to understand that death was inevitable. Despite my time in the service, I had been sheltered from the iniquities of death and dying. Here in this small Florida nursing home I found out about that part of life which is called dying.

I consider this brief glimpse into the life of an Occupational Therapist the pivotal point in my career. I took *Intro to Poetry* instead of *Anatomy and Physiology II*. Though I knew I might face a life of abject poverty, I was going to do what I loved. As a kid I had been a farmhand, a bagger, a stocker, and a cook at Golden Corral in the days before the "All You Can Eat" buffet. I had half a dozen or more jobs after the service and before I even started school. I went home and learned who my brothers were and apologized to them and my parents for disappearing to Europe for nearly a decade. It was my love for Europe and my wife, not any disaffection for them that kept me away. Observing Italian families, I learned to appreciate my own family. In America, the family unit often dissolves as children and siblings seek independent fates. Of course this isn't always true. If I learned nothing else as an aspiring academic, I did at least come to appreciate life's subtleties. Absolutes are almost always wrong.

I started New Plains Press soon after finishing grad school at Goddard and published my first book, which was almost entirely raw imagery. My wife and I wrote a book called *Remembering Sicily* which made me a US poet, finally. Then I participated in a project published under the title *Table Five*. *Table Five* features experimental, even surrealist, prose poems which were written in rotation by myself, Sue Walker (then Alabama Poet Laureate), the inimitable poet and playwright Scott Wilkerson, and artist-poet Melissa Dickson. *Hunger* is a personal project, an effort to explore my inner and outer world, my relationship with my family, my environment, and my God.

I felt compelled to bring together poems I had already written with new ones. The collection is non-linear and not especially thematic. I go from Sicily to America, from the past to the present. There are abstract-private poems that rely on reader response and may defy interpretation. I risk sentimentality and I offer words to the altar of art for the sake of art in others. There is room in poetry for these detours and indulgences.

In "Thrown to the Lions" I get a little grotesque, I suppose, but ancient life was a much tougher existence than ours:

> *Needs no knowing to hear the terrifying cries/*
> *the cracking and splintering fingernails gripping, groping,/*
> *frantically they must have clawed*

These realities and fears have been realized by peoples as late as yesterday in Ethiopia, or in the 40s in Europe, as is cited in the poem My mother-in-law never forgets to tell me of the pain of WWII, and then the ease she felt as Americans handed her candies. Though, I'm afraid, some modern dictators who have murdered thousands upon thousands, especially in Africa, have been attributed to American involvement in some form or fashion. Whether it was intentional or circumstantial seems irrelevant to me. People died for ridiculous reasons: Jewish, Muslim, Christian, black, handicapped, misunderstood and innocent bystanders. Pastor Jeffress recently analogized man's continuum of goodness as one that spans from the North to the South Pole, but the difference between God's goodness and ours is like the distance from the earth to the sun.

Someone asked me one day, "Why does God allow such atrocities to occur?" My answer was in this question: "How come there aren't a lot more atrocities, as man's heart is exceedingly wicked?" I also asked, "Why does he save any of us?" Jeffress put the same question to his audience. I invited my friend to read how in the Old Testament, God punished the Israelites and the

Egyptians who left Egypt with them, for complaining all the time. We are all of one blood (see Acts 17 about blood). In Genesis, God took Abraham to create a new nation (same blood) to be a people set aside. No one can be forced to believe these truths, that all come from God and that all deserve love, and that the human body is the sacred temple of God since the death of Christ. These are the truths I ran from all my life. Americans are idolatrous in that they worship money and themselves. None are righteous, surely, but there is a prevailing wind of change that scares me. I see death on the horizon, unless God intervenes. I will pray for this intervention because the ball is rolling out of control.

On a lighter note "Mini-Stroke" is for my precious Aunt Jackie. She had a stroke and it nearly shattered me. I drove straight away to Orlando. She has always been a gentle soul. She loves to teach kids in Sunday School, and she will make even the hardest person crack a smile. She looks the most like my grandmother, Bessie Bell Buckles Brown, another gentle soul who always cut the chickens out of feed bags for us to color. She and Jackie could hug. Jackie is a little too weak to hug like that anymore. I still remember the hugs though. Bessie, my grandmother, and my mom looked like a matching trio. That family resemblance was a delight to me. Though my Aunt never smoked, I used this opportunity to address issues that concern me in the tobacco industry and often do lead to strokes and untold deaths. I worked in tobacco fields throughout my teen years. The chemicals sprayed on the plants burned my eyes and was surely absorbed through my skin in those summer days-all that exposure just so I could wear new jeans instead of hand me downs from the Florida Sheriff's Boy's Ranch. We all have things we gripe about, yes? I didn't want to gripe, so I wrote a funny story.

I am going to stop here because I fear this exercise is futile, though I dare not keep this out of the collection. It reveals my heart and my direction in life, and will shape the press as I move forward. I hope you enjoy the book. Do not try too hard to understand. Enjoy the words I have shared as if I were sitting next to you on a cool Fall day and you are listening but you aren't... know what I mean? You can hear more that way. God be with you. And with me.

~ Johnny Summerfield
February 2014

www.ingramcontent.com/pod-product-compliance
Lightning Source LLC
LaVergne TN
LVHW021547080426
835509LV00019B/2884